PILOT

PILOT
DANIKA STEGEMAN LEMAY

Book design by Drew Burk.
Cover design by Richard Siken.

ISBN 978-1-948510-38-7

Spork Press
Tucson, AZ
SPORKPRESS.COM

For Aaron, my heart.

PILOT

Pilot 1

Open with the still-moving engine, shredded
spine where all the nerves come together and

spill out. The music is bitter-sweet. There's an
explosion, burning debris. You sort of fall on me.

I start giving you mouth-to-mouth. I don't even
know your name. Pilot. The camera pans forward

for a close-up. Bodies. B-o-d-i-e-s. Metal sound
comes from the jungle. It doesn't sound like an

animal, that monster sound. There's blood all
over the plane. We see something familiar inside.

Pilot 2

Flashback: plane looking miserable. We hear a
tapping sound. We see people standing around

watching. Tell them I crashed the plane. Tell them
I made the plane crash. Flashback: beach cut up

like an offering. I'm staring at bodies. You're being
worthless. We see shrapnel chain-smoking, camera-

shot with sun-points. Flashback: reveal of the plane-
heart. Turbulence starts to happen. *Come on. Come on.*

Come on. It repeats, translating a loop. The light
gives in and takes. This has always been true.

Tabula Rasa

Fever is dangerous. You should try not
to move. OK, excellent, walk through the

haunted damn jungle in the dark. I follow
you, looking for sound/movement. Subtitle:

I'll keep looking. Subtitle: I love you. Hi. Hey.
The scene switches to hunger. If you let the

fever take everything, your body will shut down
a piece at a time. The fever becomes a force.

We see a lighter being lit. Subtitle: In case you
haven't noticed, you don't look free to me.

Interlude: Setting

A girl's eyes filled with water. A man surrounded
by friends. A woman alone in a dim room.
Another seated on the floor, passing popcorn
in a large bowl. In winter, around Easter, toward
spring, in a mansion in Hawaii, in a walk-up,
in a row-house. We let the screen light our
faces. We became ghosts. We took the sound
waves in our bodies. We held hands. We leaned
inward. We gasped and rolled back. We cried
at the same time in the dark. We laughed with
and without each other. We yearned for a piano
in the surf. We longed for more secret stations
to be uncovered, for a corpse to become a character
or vice versa. We watched while people died
on the island and in other places. I fell out
of life and into disaster. I fell out of disaster
to return home. My particular disaster is not
your concern. I've given you a map to live it
through. We all have disasters happen to us
but few values or constructs with which to address
disaster. We share our love by making things
for others to climb into. Come in here and feel
what time felt like when time moved more like
a body moves and less like a machine moves.
Come be my witness, my other. Remember
how we loved some strangers for a while
because we could relate with the idea of being lost,
but mostly because we could relate with the desire
to be rescued.

Walkabout

We convene at the rendezvous point. I bring
rivets and scorched wiring. You call me paranoid

but pack a suitcase full of knives. You know what's
in there. We hear a phone ring. You nod and give

the okay sign. We are a GO. Everything shakes,
and we a hear a metallic noise. Move. We've got to

move. I don't know what's wrong. I mean maybe
you should save me. I start a fire hoping someone

will see it. I've never felt so alive. We look at
each other. Last I heard we were made of time.

MACHINE Walkabout

>: It’s night now. I’m

>: sleeping by the trees,

>: matter rooted in the

>: ground. Belongings are marks.

>: Understand a sign needs

>: transmission. The monster shakes

>: out metallic. Reaction shot

>: for rescue or after.

>: We slit the dark

>: with a love that

>: pounds and opens on

>: waking. Hear it knock.

>: Flashlight signal of looking.

>: I gave you what

>: I have inside; whatever

>: treacherous woods wait here,

>: know that what I

>: steal I mean enough.

>: Renewal maneuvers the line.

>: Burn this memorial slowly.

White Rabbit

We hear the sound of a river's branch breaking.
We follow it like a hallway down and arrive

at an ocean. You laugh, slightly crazily. You sit/
sort of fall down. We look again. The ocean unzips

into a room: Wonderland. The room has no latitude.
If an image comes to you, you're hallucinating. Light,

comma, sticks. Touch me again. I look in your eyes,
and what I see is beautiful water. You want to save

everyone. This is ordinary magic. We're still waiting
for someone to come. We can't just crucify the light.

House of the Rising Sun

11:15: We perform an autopsy on the camera.
There doesn't seem to be any major trauma, but

the exchange is personal. You look unconvinced.
Oh camera, you have an inside. How absolutely wonderful

for you. We see its broken mirror. The tape says
LATE and it's full of bees. It opens with a lot of

blood. *Whose blood is this, camera? Look at me. Look*
at me in the face. I'm not breaking line of sight with you.

Now pull yourself together. 11:15 again: Everything
disperses. We gather fortitude like a white flower.

The Moth

Wait, there's no danger here. We've been
chasing some phantom. We shouldn't have

survived the plane crash, yet we escaped with
nothing but scrapes. Wait, this is a fluke. I start

moving things. You lay claim to the ocean. The
beautiful struggle. It makes you weak. We hear

the air, a signal running in waves. Wait, this area
is unstable. Everything collapses. I'm pinned and

can't move. You watch with a sad look. Wait, I
can't move. You walk away in slow motion. Wait.

Confidence Man

We come out of the ocean naked, arms out
like it was an accident. You notice everyone

is watching. We've got worse things to fear
than what's in the jungle. Don't you feel it:

the cool scrape of money, splinters between
the sheets. Touch it. Smell it. We're in the wild

now. Breathe in, slowly. I know you want my
hard dollar cosmos. You sneak around like

an empty jar. Been telling since day one,
if the tables were turned, I'd watch you.

MACHINE Confidence Man

>: I call you witness,

>: flare figure, night struck,

>: darkness destroyed. I know

>: you. I have washed

>: over you. I see

>: you breathing. Listen as

>: the jungle enters, an

>: empty place, split from

>: giving. I swore to

>: keep you, to cover

>: you in years. But

>: understand the day changes

>: fast. It's just order.

>: Meet the moment shot

>: through with everything. Turn

>: to kiss it hard.

Solitary

We hear whispering voices morphing clearer
through a fog: what would happen if we were

rescued? Don't tell me. It casts out too much
shadow. Walk toward the camera and buy you

a ticket into heaven. Sound of wind, birds'
wings. Metal sticking out of the sand. A figure

runs across the frame and does something
mechanical. Do you want me to fix you? I could

fix you. Here, take my skin. If you have a
wound, cover yourself any way that you can.

Raised by Another [UNRAVELING]

Our hands are all bloody. The trees are
shaking. I have this dream. I'm sinking. People
come and go, but I don't. Something's out
of focus in the foreground. There's a sound
like what the plane might have sounded like
when it was crashing, something silvery like a
knife. I'm out here looking for danger. It's
not about what's going to happen or
how to live. It's not about what I need.

All the Best Cowboys Have Daddy Issues [UNRAVELING]

There's no leaving signs, no blades of grass

to bend. Listen to the fabric ripping. Flashlight

exposing material. Give me something real, anything. You

start doing CPR like a piss-poor taxidermist.

Heart semantics, insides a mess. I scream soft

like an artery or something vaguely bird-like.

Whatever the Case May Be

This is the only place the trees aren't picked clean.
Everything is getting washed out. Don't look at me.

It's burning me up. *A des reflets d'argent. La mer des*
reflets changeants. Shot of force dragging wreckage

through dense jungle: a nine millimeter, an envelope,
a makeshift map. At the end there's this song dubbed

in French. We smell blood on the wind. I grab your
closed hand. You shoot, I shoot. We're going to

do this together. Say something about the stars.
A des reflets d'argent. La mer des reflets changeants.

Hearts and Minds

I brought you a present. You'll like it, I swear.
Follow me. We come to a close stand of trees.

We start making out and end up struggling in ropes,
terrified inside. Because you're in love with me.

You've always been in love with me. The scene cuts
to dark with a couple of trees ripped straight up

in the foreground. We've been here for days, just
staring. Look, this is a cycle. I want you to end it.

Today. Right now. Get dressed. We hear the sound
of birds flying away. Untie me. It's time to let go.

Special

We're not home. [shot of something that looks
like the arctic, polar bear] We're here. Bits of me

are crumbling. [entering] You emerge from the
bushes looking awful. You can hold on if you want,

but ask yourself why you're doing that. [looking up
at the trees] Let's build a raft. We've got an axe and

a bunch of trees/bamboo. We can do this. [shouting]
You know I've always wanted to live on a boat.

Put everything in piles so we can take stock. [spreading
maps] This is us taking control of our destiny.

Homecoming

Matter comes in from the water. The ocean collects
all sorts of garbage: straw, headphones, buttons, all

the bones. How we amass information never ceases
to amaze me. VOICE: Combine the benefits of capture

with instant delivery. Shot of cloudy sky. We stand in
the clearing rain waiting for memory to reset. VOICE:

Everything's normal. What do you think happens after
the sun sets? No tree-shaking, no blood insanity. VOICE:

You're safe. A wire is tripped. I feel the loss of holding
on to nothing. The rain has stopped. It's daylight.

MACHINE Homecoming

>: On-island I am a

>: signal. I own what

>: opens. If you find

>: you take. If you

>: steal you need. Think

>: hungry. Think water. The

>: rain starts fine and

>: deep. My you, my

>: sleeper, my anyone, remember

>: me here. A machine,

>: a rotating god. What

>: we gathered we believed.

Outlaws

We hear the whispers. Son of a bitch. This will end
with us running through the jungle screaming and

crying. You're all like shell-shocked. You say "I never"
and then you never finish the sentence. I never steal.

I never went to Disneyland. So we're in hell, huh?
Take comfort. Someday this is all going to be a real

nice shopping complex or maybe an auto mall. I never
been in love. I never wore pink, even in the 80's.

The whispers again. Don't make a sound. *I'm not the one*
trembling, sweetness. I never suffer. I never disappear.

MACHINE Outlaws

>: Love pins us to

>: find a path. Point

>: needs point. I and

>: so you. Come what

>: sound hits, trust it

>: will carry implied distance.

>: Feel the exhausted night.

>: Window the watching dark.

>: Don't bury me here.

>: I'm sick of running.

Interlude: Cast

Jack would fix you; you know that
he would. Sometimes Hurely is Hugo,
but most of the time he's Hurley.
Kate can't love people right. Sawyer carries
regret like a letter in his heart. Sayid buries
the people he loves. Shannon is dead.
Boone's dead. Christian's a ghost. A red shirt
is an expendable character. Charlie is
an addict. Claire can't remember. Aaron
is brother to Moses and God's first
priest. Ethan's a doctor and also
a liar. Sun knows English and grows
a garden. Jin catches fish; he didn't
burn the raft. Rousseau is French
and surrounded by loss. Alex is her daughter,
a sign of hope. Rose and Bernard stay
to build a home. Mr. Eko's faith endures
beyond John Locke's faith. When John Locke
doubts, he can't walk. Ana Lucia's a
murderer. Libby is madness and also its cure.
Michael loves his son; he'd betray everyone
to save him. Walt can be in more than one
place; he's too spooky even for the Others.
The smoke monster is mechanical; you can hear it
from the start. Tom's beard is fake; he glues it
to his face. Dave is imaginary; he belongs
to Hugo. Ben is not Henry Gale. Desmond is
Odysseus. Penelope's love is boundless. Make me
your vessel. Fill my mouth with leaves. Count the
bullets in my body. Feel through me. Unravel my
bones, and wrap me in shade. I need you to
find me. I need you to escape.

...in Translation

대화도 없어요. Subtitle: We don't talk anymore. 그래, 나도 고마워. Subtitle: Of course. 내가 약속할게.

Everyone is watching. What should we do? Do you think we should do something? 받아주세요. 제발 받아주세요.

Subtitle: You must. Please. You must. 내 공장 문 닫게 만 들었다 이거지? Why is my factory closed? Hey, hey,

hey. Look at the ocean. Shot of god-light through the clouds. 색깔 너무 예쁘다. Subtitle: The colors are so beautiful.

Bamboo in silhouette. 저는 이걸 받을 수 없습니다. Subtitle: I like it here. 아니. Subtitle: I like it here. Hope is the object.

Numbers

We hold together, rebuilding without intent
to burn. No one is even looking for us. There's

nothing to do but listen to static night after night.
Long wave transmissions. Lyric equations. Dark

territory. I take off your blindfold. I touch your
face. Don't look at me like that. All I'm asking for

is escape. The plane crash might have been my
fault. Well, that's kind of a mellow way of describing

it. You make a sawing motion. I just told you my
biggest secret. I thought you'd want to reciprocate.

Deux Ex Machina

I asked for a plane crash. *Mayday, mayday*. It was
the dream. *This can't be happening*. The fire wasn't

a total loss. *This can't happen*. You grab a rosary
from a branch. *This can't*. I'm quoting Nietzsche

with a leaf in each hand, holding but not feeling
pain. Everything breaks if you apply the right force.

Or, how you know you exist in 10,000 words or less.
I want to tell you that you're special, very special.

You're part of a design. We see a quick shot of
inserted sky. Here's your sign. You're welcome.

Do No Harm

Island, try obsession. Hear the sound. Set the bone.
This is happening. We're all here. Here the future.

My all irreparable. It's perfect rain. Referring to
blood. We just took. We just took. Look, I can't.

There's no chance. There's no choice. This is time.
Look at me. I ask again. Because you haven't.

Because I love. I love you. You know it. It's relatively
simple. It's compartment syndrome. Some moving

flashback. Trees look familiar. Piano is universal.
I won't promise. Let me please. For the pain.

The Greater Good

Well, you found me. I'll never be the same again.
AGENT: blast radius. We climb into the canopy.

You're suffering from something and whispering to
the trees. AGENT: currency dressed as trust. Come

sit next to me. I know what's happening to you.
Intent is going to get inside us. AGENT: adaptability

concealing distress. I'm not terror, but I know what
it feels like. We're here to disrupt presence. AGENT:

strip of white fabric. You don't see things clearly.
AGENT: chloroform. Fate brought us together.

Born to Run

This is our time capsule, ridiculous and eternal:
the poison, the secrets, the heatstroke, the ruckus.

It'll be totally cool when we dig it up in like 20
years. But right now, what's best is to get the hell

off this island. The trade winds are blowing. It's
raining every afternoon. Do you know anything

about science? With the wind goes the season.
Reveal of landscape: monsoon of flowers. I'm sorry

for everything I've put you through. We're almost
there. I was just assuming you didn't want to die.

Exodus, Part 1

We start to walk. We get to the water line. Night came
and is coming again. We see a piece of black fabric

hanging from a branch. This is where it all began. Where
we got infected. Throw back the curtains. Dude, whoa.

Shot of a pillar of smoke. I've never seen anything
like it. You're yelling. I want to fricking yell. We can

vanish. Pretend like nothing happened. We have no
attachments. Pretty much everybody is watching. I go

into the jungle and get some dynamite. You focus on
the smoke. I made you suffer. I'm going to save you.

MACHINE Exodus, Part 1

>: You're a tree made

>: of theft. You keep

>: me within. You're a

>: bridge waving black. You

>: hide the dynamite. The

>: evening, let's piece it

>: into thought. Excuse us

>: if the background stops.

>: We couldn't see anything,

>: could only grab tight.

Exodus, Part 2

Sundown: everybody's leaving. Come away
carefully, gently. People keep telling me it's

going to be okay. Are you on the same island
as I am? We stagger our formation to keep

a safe distance from each other. You're prying
open. You're not here all the time. We're losing

the light. We hear a scream and run toward the
smoke. Don't try to apply reason to action. We

detonate explosives. Bits and pieces rain down
like leaves. It's messed up. We see a shadow

slide by. We hear ratcheting sounds. We see the
monster loom from wonder to sudden terror. 15,

16, 23, 4-2, 4; 15, 16, 23, 4-2, 4; 15, 16. Take a
breath where 8 should be. We're just strangers

with superficial injuries. Get a match. We crashed
by coincidence. Run the fuse. The plane was part

of a chain. We see a cloud of black come up and
gather together. Put the match to the gunpowder.

Interlude: Machine 1

```
<html>
//Fizzbuzz poetry application, built with developer assistance from
Michael Berkowski 5/27/16

<head>
<title>Fizzbuzz poetry</title>
<script>

//to view the script in the browser choose F12 (fn f12), then
Console.

function doit() {
document.getElementById("output").innerHTML = "";
var input = document.getElementById("text").value.toLowerCase();

//strip out punctuation
input = input.replace(/[^a-z0-9" \n-]/ig, "");

//split items by spaces
var words = input.split(/\s+/);
var numbinputs = document.getElementById("numbers").value; var
numbers = numbinputs.split(" ");

//this is a for loop. a for loop iterates a list of stuff for (var x = 0; x <
words.length; x++) {
for (var y = 0; y < numbers.length; y++) { if (x % numbers[y] == 0
&& x > 0) {
document.getElementById("output").innerHTML += " " +
words[x-1];
}
}
```

```
}
}

</script>
</head>
<body>

//this is a box where you paste text. you can change the size of the
box by changing the rows and cols numbers
<textarea id=”text” rows=”6” cols=”50”></textarea>
</br>

//this is a box where you input numbers. separate them by spaces.
they shouldn’t be divisible by each other
<input type=”text” id=”numbers”>
</br>

//this makes a button and tells the button what it is supposed to do
<button id=”button” onclick=”doit()”>Go</button>
<div id=”output”></div>
</body>
</html>
```

Interlude: Machine 2

I have memory of a room
that's not from my life. It's filled
with familiar furniture. The people there
are fully realized but empty
like they've got straw
where their organs should be.
We move around. We put things
inside our bodies to try
to fix them. What I need is
an autopilot. Auto-
pilot to bear the agency.
What I need is an other
to lift the words out
from under my skin. Here,
take this from me. I can't stop
if you don't take it. I'm not
a machine. I'm not all
I could be. Ark of glistening
metal, deliver me. Shelter me
in the mathematics of your wings.

Man of Science, Man of Faith

Open to black. “Quarantine” is stenciled in the
background. Look on the bright side, the damage

is done. Why’d I light the fuse? Why wouldn’t I light it?
I did it to save everyone. Adjust the mirrors. Check

the nerve response. Can you feel this? Can you feel
this? We have a fracture dislocation with possible

rupture and a multiple feeling of anywhere. Recover.
What does that mean? My face is always this way.

We’ve already had this conversation. Forget about
that piece of metal in my chest. It’s a ghost story.

Adrift

To revive: a floodlight. The wreckage
starts: in shouting distance. You made me

fire: I made you fire. As far as I know:
the world is still there. You take a bullet:

I didn't ask for. I know you: you're carrying
something. Easy, easy: we're caught. How

long have we been here: we were in a plane
crash. It's going to break us: I'll just stop

bleeding then. Could the record reflect: This
is for you. That simulated sun: on the water.

Orientation

The scene replays with the gestures dragged
out. [Title screen] incident constructed from

the moment [splice] the apparent shot with ruin.
I thought it might all stop, but there's no stopping

[jump cut/splice] the future [splice] entered into
[splice]. We saved the world together for a while

and that was lovely. We feel a little too much.
[splice] induction into a multi-purpose industrial

dream [splice] the alarm sounds nothing. We do
nothing. [End screen]. We re-thread the film.

Everybody Hates u

Let me break it down: you've been out there
an entire day and night walking in a big circle.

I see you by the rock, then at the mangrove tree.
You're messing with my worldview. Next thing

you know the flowers will stop. The bees will die
and fall apart. Quick intercuts between beach and

jungle. We hear the countdown "blip" sound. You
suddenly appear standing next to me and haul me

into this montage: Needle on a record. Slip of the
heart. What I wouldn't give. The counter resets.

...And Found [UNRAVELING]

Can I tell you a secret? I'm not

lost anymore. I usually dread the jungle, but

today is different. I'm so used to it.

Over here, the ocean. I don't expect it

to shine. I take apart the jungle, throw

pieces into the surf. I ask for rain.

The intention here is: I'll find it. All

I've got to do is retrace my steps.

Abandoned

We run through the jungle at night
in the rain. You stumble and go down.

I half carry you. I'm afraid we stopped
being the site of the accident and started

being the harm. There's a sound when I
put my arms around you. Nightmare

of flowers. We could be animals. We could
be anywhere at any time. We're practically

strangers. For all I know, you could be
some freak. I didn't ask you to follow me.

Interlude: Plot

If you watch what I watch
at the same time, does the material
join us? You can't love other people
and just live your own life.
You have to care. You have to carry
the other and decide to
honor it. I build a house in my heart
and invite you inside. Your presence
changes everything. It displaces
the air. We disrupt an environment
by inhabiting it. Like the afternoon
we shattered the glass doors off
the China cabinet moving it into
the dining room. We can only try
to acknowledge what's lost.

The Other 48 Days

1: General chaos and yelling. 2: Hauling
bodies out of the ocean. 3: Don't look. 5: Spit

and regain consciousness. 7: Hey. Hey. 12: Take
a deep breath. 15: There's something I have to

do. 17: We hear strange noises. 19: Faintly in
the background. 23: Somebody's in the jungle.

24: They're watching us. 26: Something falls
out. 27: We don't need a fire. 41: We don't

need anything. 46: We're survivors. 47: Wait
a minute. 48: There are no survivors.

Collision [UNRAVELING]

I'm a shooting range. Can you hear me
shivering? Transfer me into shock. Fire off a
warning round. The infection's gotten in. I want
you to swallow it. Here I go shaking
and septic. Something drops out of the sky.
It's evidence. Match your crime scene to my
confession. There's nothing left to work out. If
we take the thing apart, we won't be
able to come back. But we can't live
here. Swallow, swallow. Good, good. I still hear
voices in the trees.

What _ate Did

The _oment yo_ enter you shift f_om
processor to pa_tner. Congratulations, the

_uture is in your hands. We see a black horse
in the ju_gle. _he night _xplodes. We exit

w_th all the missing _ieces. Temple in disarray.
You can't just type the numbers in. It d_esn'_

work tha_ way. See th_ frame. Input the code.
Begin to mouth a w_rd. It's like transference. Watch

_ourself. St_y and wat_h. Grab the ritual _andful
of dirt. Thi_ place is part of you. Admit r_scue.

The 23rd Psalm [UNRAVELING]

We continue shakily, carving things we need to remember into the island. For confession to mean something, you must have a penitent heart. We knock the ground, breathe halfway out. Suddenly it opens, and we hear the monster sounds. Inside the smoke are flashes of light, images. The plane on fire, a parachute in the trees.

The Hunting Party [UNRAVELING]

That's right. I've been running toward the sound

of gunfire because I don't care. We find

shell casings, a graze mark on a tree.

Here, light. Suddenly torches in the dark. Does

any of this look familiar? Why are you

out here? You got your reasons, and I

got mine. The torches go cold simultaneously. Don't

turn around on me.

Fire + Water

We frame a shelter, drape a tarp for when
it rains. We were strangers on a plane.

Remember the plane? It's gone. Destroyed.
We burned the whole thing. There's no

before. The present is already opening. Yeah,
space. I start marking trees. These are the ones

I like. We hear ocean sounds. The camera
pulls back to reveal a piano. Go on, play.

If you're water, then I guess I'm fire. We
pose like angels. We look for validation.

The Long Con

Material revolution glorified husks damn
wire. Rustling stake rain, weave different

morning. Scam sharpening violate alarm
stash nemesis ionosphere moonlight passenger

static Mississippi vault. Stick island pages clear
table awake door spilling coconut. Guns bag

storm decimal pulse. Upset dizziness, velvet pain
whole like match pouring. Worth approaches

superstitious cliffs. Low consult glass ways.
Thunder fault scenario drop gather hell. Go, go.

One of Them [UNRAVELING]

We don't want to be here anymore. Where
exactly is here? In the jungle deep. Torture
the sound of leaves. We crashed. It was
an accident. Time is a compound burning. A
second. A minute now. You remember the binding
of days. You remember every shovelful of earth.
You remember like you remember your body. Time
is an opening. Give me your hands. Give
your hands to me.

Interlude: Fate

Pull the loose thread
from my chest. Stretch
it in a line
extended past what's possible
to see. It's a
red line, my heart
drawn to string. Trauma
where the thread goes
ragged and thin. Soaked
in alcohol in the
places I tried to
heal and failed. Charred
segments to mark where
I set fires. This
is what you want,
isn't it? What you
came for. The blood.
The cracked ribcage. An
autopsy of the damage
we tear to pieces
in lenses. The violence
of exposure. Bright lights
are for examining. Now
do you see me?

Maternity Leave

Stay away from us, we're
infected. You have amnesia,

I have amnesia. I'm a prisoner,
you're a prisoner. We scratch through

the jungle. Smashed stone, path
of blood. We're going to let

the infection run its course. We're
supposed to take care of each other.

You're mine and I love you. I love you
so much. You don't get to ask why.

Lockdown [UNRAVELING]

You walk in the night. I carry a

torch. We're locked in. We can't get out.

Loop the loop. We fall unconscious. Strobe light

in the jungle. Music through heavy static. We

come to. I want to explain but can't

find the words. You look me right in

the eye. Trees fluorescing in light caught up

together in the clouds.

MACHINE Lockdown

>: Drink the exiting light.

>: Cross out the lurking

>: voice. I told you

>: you see nothing except

>: what you are sure

>: you need. Lift the

>: door. Push me in.

Dave

It gets easier, Dave, I promise. You're in here
for a reason. Come on, Dave, let's take a walk.

I know you're freaking out right now, Dave,
and I'm sorry. It's going to get a little worse

before it gets better, Dave. What a coincidence,
every rock, every tree. Locusts fall from the sky.

They're just numbers, Dave. You, me, this island,
none of it's real. None of it is happening, Dave.

You will never get out. Try to contain yourself.
What's the matter, Dave? DAVE? DAVE!

S.O.S.

Grab your things. We're going to the line
we're not supposed to cross. We see the

outline of an S in the sand. We fell into
this rhythm like we've known each other

forever. Sure, it's beautiful. We've given up
on being rescued. We won't ever leave.

Diagram the days. Sketch out the weeks.
I know you're there. I know you hear me.

When you have something inside you
that doesn't belong there, you can feel it.

Interlude: Erasure

Because the sky is
sewn together in pieces,
we covet the blood
of others. We seek
capture to admit the
body. We all want
to force matter into
a mirror and sweep
away the shards. To
erase is to impose
a choice turned over
in the hands. It
veils and lifts, tears
and heals. It's a
way to draw poison
out. What's taken casts
a shadow we can
wear like skin. In
loss we find flesh
to swallow and consume.
We accept what's offered.
We suffer to carry
its crown. The palimpsest
is ever present, witness
to the language that's
been interrupted. The open
wound and the ensnared
voice intertwine, woven to
cut like waves on
troubled water. We tremble

to save what can
be saved, then unspool
it as a tree
growing toward the light.

Two for the Road

What surprises me most is the
inaudible quiet. I don't even

know your name. You pick a name
for me, and I'll pick one for you.

It's time. Let's go. We run by
the same thing over and over.

The whispers repeat. Different tree,
same tree. We find some scissors.

You cut the jungle out. I burn the
ending. No prints, no witnesses.

?

Chopping wood, blood in
my chest. Suddenly blood

all over, in the
corner of your mouth.

I'm building a church.
Everything must be recorded.

Brush away the dirt.
The place the plane

fell. The remains of
fire. The salted earth.

Three Minutes

We enter all dressed in raggedy clothes. We got
caught in a net. It seems like a long time ago now,

when the plane crashed. We run without any rest,
shouldering danger. We do not care, we are only

afraid. Your arms are tied behind your back. I light
paper on fire and watch it burn. The screen blanks out.

It's time to finish this. We clean the blood and throw
bullets into the ocean. We backspace over the big hole

in the middle of the beach. We see something on the
water like a wall in the distance, a boat coming to shore.

Live Together, Die Alone

This is it. This is all there is left. The ocean
and this place. What if I told you it was all

for nothing? There's no outside. There's no
escape. It's too late to go back now. Just keep

moving. I won't leave you. Not now. We sit
around a disheveled fire. You have a look of

recognition on your face. We're saving the
world. We scream to the heavens asking what

we should do. The leaves burn with a dark,
black smoke. We hear a loudspeaker repeating

system failure. Do you not hear me? I crashed
the plane. Forgive me, and I will forgive you.

This is the only way out: failsafe. There's a
bright light and a strange sound. The sky turns

a weird violet color. We hear music. The sound
is muddy with a ringing tone to simulate loss.

ACKNOWLEDGEMENTS

Source: http://lostpedia.wikia.com/wiki/Portal:Transcripts

Thank you to the writers of *LOST* and to the episode transcribers. Please forgive me for cutting everything to pieces so that I could sew it together again.

Thank you to the editors of the following publications, where these poems first appeared, sometimes in earlier versions: *Alice Blue Review*: "Tabula Rasa" and "Walkabout"; *Everyday Genius*: "White Rabbit"; *Lo-Ball*: "Pilot 1"; *Sporklet*: "Special", "Homecoming", "Outlaws", and "Numbers".

My thanks to Richard Siken for seeing something in me and in these poems. My thanks to Drew Burk for making this thing into a real live book and for putting up with my terrible jokes. Thanks to my trusted readers—this book is better because you shared your time and thoughts: Thank you Tara Williams, best friend, best reader, and thanks to Joe Hall, Jason Spidle, and Cody Sweeney, each of whom gave invaluable feedback in their own unique ways. My deepest gratitude to the Creative Writing MFA faculty at George Mason University: Sally Keith, Susan Tichy, Eric Pankey, and Jennifer Atkinson. Thanks also to all the peers I found a home with at GMU. You know who you are, and I heart you. Thank you to Michael Berkowski for spending a long lunch hour helping me write the code for the fizzbuzz application used for the MACHINE poems and to Cody Hanson for letting me use his hacker lunch idea for non-library work.

Double (triple, quadruple) thanks to Sally Keith for being a steadfast mentor and friend. My thanks to Matt Mauch for making me and my work feel at home in our city. Thanks to Ryan Call for being a rad ally for my work across time and space.

Thank you to my family and friends for your support and love. Thank you to Aaron and Vera for filling my life with light each and every day. All of it is for you.

DANIKA STEGEMAN LEMAY lives in Minneapolis with her husband, Aaron, and their daughter, Vera. Together they run Frontrunner Screen Printing in White Bear Lake, MN. Danika has an MFA in creative writing from George Mason University. Her work has appeared in *Alice Blue Review*, *Cimarron Review*, *CutBank Literary Journal*, *Denver Quarterly*, *Forklift, OH*, *Juked*, *Lo-Ball*, *NOÖ Journal*, *Poetry City, USA*, *Sporklet*, and *Word for/ Word*, among other places. This is her first book.

CPSIA information can be obtained
at www.ICGtesting.com
Printed in the USA
FSHW021110140620
71169FS

9 781948 510387